Prayer for the Dead:
Collected Haibun & Tanka Prose

Prayer for the Dead:
Collected Haibun & Tanka Prose

By Margaret Lane Dornaus

Singing Moon Press
2016

First Printing: 2016

ISBN 978-0-9982112-0-6

Singing Moon Press
Ozark, AR 72949

Cover design by Jacquelyn Stuber

Cover photo: "Handprints," Mutawintji National Park cave, New South Wales, Australia, by Margaret Dornaus

Distributed by: www.lulu.com

Dedicated to the memory

of

Larry Chapman Kelly

(January 17, 1954—November 20, 2014)

and to all those who have danced

before the firelight to find their way home to me

Contents

Foreword ix

Prayer for the Dead 13

Afterword 96

Acknowledgements.. 103

Publication Credits 105

About the Author 107

Foreword

As we grow older we become increasingly interested in our own individual heritage, wanting to learn more than ever who has gone before us in order to link hands with the past. *Prayer for the Dead*, a collection of haibun and tanka prose by Margaret Dornaus, is a perfect example of this attempt at linkage, trying to remember, trying not to forget, trying to memorialize a family loved one, a friend, a lover:

> heat lightning the way your hand rests on mine

This ancestry is our heritage and we are (though we may not know it) part and parcel of a plethora of individuals who have gone before us. We are a montage of that which we have inherited: a familiar smile, the color of the eyes and hair, the haunting laugh all combine to make up who we are. We are always and ever defined by those who have gone before us.

> handprints
>
> on the wall of a cave
>
> all the ancestors
>
> dancing before firelight
>
> finding their way home to me

Prayer for the Dead is a touching tribute to those individuals who have defined the poet by their existence: mother, father, grandparents, siblings, husband and friends. We are all defined not only by our loved ones but by events in history, houses in the homeland, a stranger on the bus; all of it comprise the poet's psyche.

        names of the dead . . .

        for a moment the fog

        parts and rises

The poet—as translator of thoughts and feelings—takes us with her on a journey of memory through time and space (Italy, Australia, Germany):

        cobblestones . . .

        a klezmer song drifts

        through ancient streets

Her ancestor's blood runs through her own veins and the poet is connected by this invisible yet tangible link; she knows in the deep blue vein of veins the image of the ancestor's face is just like her own.

        passover . . .

        a gypsy moth circles

        the candle's flame

We share, though briefly, her impressions of relationships which have marked her own individual growth as a poet and as a human being. In this light, we come to understand the poet better, carried along by her beautiful, telling words. It would be difficult to imagine the world without Dornaus' poetry; it is pure inspiration:

north by northeast

a splinter of geese flies

far from this heat

I too ponder

how I'll leave this earth

What is remarkable about this collection is the poet's ability to rise above the pain of existence when confronted with the loss of a loved one. She is able to crystallize each significant moment into a treasured keepsake which sparkles in the dark. She then graciously shares this keepsake with the reader shedding light on us all:

meteor shower . . .

we name each falling star

for the loved ones

who pass again before us

this bright cloudless morning

When all is said and done the poet speaks for us in a vibrantly clear tone sharing on this road of life her wisdom, her words:

another setback

on this road I travel

without you . . .

I try to imagine

my place in the world

Margaret Dornaus' new collection *Prayer for the Dead* is a significant addition to the haibun and tanka prose community. We can all be thankful that her beautiful poetry has indeed found its way home:

particle of light . . .

the gentle blurring of hands

when we wave farewell

—Marjorie Buettner, award-winning author, *Some Measure of Existence: Collected Haibun*

Prayer for the Dead

years from now

I promise to remember

how you looked that night

alone on the verandah

holding moonlight in your hands

Dreamtime

One day the Rainbow Serpent wakes from a dream to create the earth and all its inhabitants. Grass. Flowers. Trees. Frogs. Birds. Emus. Kangaroos. Wallabies. Rivers and streams. Then she makes laws for all to obey, saying, "Those who keep my laws will be given human form. Those who don't will turn to stone."

handprints

on the wall of a cave . . .

all the ancestors

dancing before firelight

finding their way home to me

hide and seek the ring around her memory

Party People

Late enough. Alone in my bed I listen to sounds drifting through open doors and windows. Muffled laughter. Snippets of speech. A high pitch. A low. The clink of ice cubes on cut-glass. A fork or knife against a spoon. The scratch of a record needle sinking deep into a groove. The rustle of skirts as they brush against trousers. A pat from a hand. A jab from an elbow. A hiccup. A belch. A pinch. A sneeze. The simultaneous snap of fingers.

On my wall, shadows morph into monsters. Venetian blinds transform into the bars of a prison. A summer breeze enters my room without knocking. I jump up and tiptoe to the second-floor landing. For a glimpse into a world of chiffon and pearls. And smoke rings. And charm bracelets of gold and silver that jangle to the distant leitmotif of another time and place.

campfire song

. . . mother's note tucked

inside my bedroll

Super-8

My father's voice is rich and deep as he keeps up his stream of commentary. There's the Eiffel Tower, girls. There's the Place de la Concorde. That's Paris, the City of Light, at night. He is speechless only once, when the film speeds ahead to the forgotten image of a young brunette posed before a sidewalk café. Her hair flips up in perfect symmetry on each side of her delicate face. And she is wearing a smile that can only be described as winsome.

jump cut . . .

the Mediterranean

floods the paper screen

A second later, my mother is snapping her fingers to wake me. My father hushes her, picks me up, and carries me to my room. Alone, I cast the names of foreign places out on whispered speech, breaking each word into syllables, each syllable into sounds; curling and uncurling my tongue until the strangeness wears off, until the names become as familiar as my own.

shadow dance

all the places I have

yet to see

The Mother Tongue

My great-grandfather spoke German. A kind of German, anyway. A strange, sing-song dialect passed to me through my father. Hand-me-down words. Holy words, trotted out for special occasions when my father's frustration level reached a certain untranslatable pitch. To my untrained ears, these vaguely-sounding yet undeniably taboo Anglo-Saxon phrases were nothing if not marvelous. The intention of the words—to intimidate, to silence—was lost on me. Their strangeness, their foreignness, is what I wanted to capture, to swallow whole and to regurgitate over and over.

Say it again, I'd cry. And like a dutiful child, my father would repeat for me the words that had cowed him when he himself was a child. *Again.* And soon we would both be smiling, and laughing.

elderberry wine . . .

the dizzying aftertaste

of long-lost words

Verboten

My mother tells me of my father's grandmother. How Bertha recounted her trip to America. Reliving the voyage as an old woman. Describing the effects of the rolling sea. Of the nausea she experienced as a young woman, heavy with her first child, no more than a child herself, at seventeen. At the time, my mother thought it odd, funny even, that Der Ma could have recalled an incident that had occurred more than half a century earlier as if she were speaking of a journey made only yesterday.

old wives' tales

we exchange our stories

with the wind

"Perhaps," my mother says suddenly, "you come by your gifts naturally." She is speaking now of language, not of memory. "Der Ma was a linguist," she adds with a flourish. It is an old, high compliment, passed down through the generations of my family.

But I am not a linguist, I want to say. Not like Der Ma. I know a little French, a little Spanish, a little unutterable German, but I don't deserve such a title. To be known by such a title . . . *What must that be?*

forbidden words

on the tip of my tongue . . .

her six-pointed star

Prayer for the Dead

The ruins of a medieval castle stand on its outskirts. The River Úhlava runs through it. It's ringed by the Böhmerwald. This much I know from guidebooks, but my pen-pal quickly gets to the heart of our ancestors' village. "In the old days," Ragnar writes, "Jews lived there."

cobblestones . . .

a klezmer song drifts

through ancient streets

Ragnar sends me eight 5x7 black and whites: four snapped around town; four of the old Jewish cemetery—a long view of the muddy field he trekked through with the farmers' dogs barking at his heels; two closer views of headstones—some upright, others overturned; the last, a stone engraved with Hebrew. "It seems very likely," Ragnar adds suddenly, "that our great-grandfathers knew each other."

saying grace—

the cantor's voice rises

in a minor key

Years later I decipher the name engraved on the last picture's tombstone. Moshe. Son of Meier. He was, his tombstone says, "upright and pious." His name was Moshe.

passover . . .

a gypsy moth circles

the candle's flame

mummy painting the young girl's eyes wide open

Goethe's Oak

All that remains of his tree today is a stump. A tombstone-like column engraved with the words *Goethe Eiche* near the base of the scarred trunk's roots. The monument, to a man who valued reason and beauty, seems at once sacred and unholy, for it lies just outside the doors to one of the twentieth century's grisliest nightmares: a preserved crematorium that was an integral part of the Nazi concentration camp known as Buchenwald.

What if the limits of our individuality allow for knowledge of the worst at the exclusion of the "most excellent"? I wish I could ask Goethe for his opinion on such extreme dichotomy; instead, I find myself sitting down to dinner with my fellow travelers.

It's a charming Hofbrau we're treated to on our last night in Weimar, but I have no appetite for either food or company. At one point, our host for the evening realizes that I've neither touched my food nor entered into conversation. After talking non-stop in his native tongue to our guide, he suddenly leans over to apologize for his rudeness. "I should be speaking in English," he says.

> death camp
>
> the charred remains
>
> of Goethe's tree

Among Strangers

"Germany unnerves me," I tell him, "but this is Berlin. Berlin's different."

"Are you sure?" he asks.

"Let me show you," I say, before taking him to the places I witnessed by myself from the close quarters of a sightseeing van. There's the sculpture garden near graffiti-splattered tenements that were home to many of the city's pre-war Jews. And the silver-and-gold dome of Berlin's rebuilt *Neue* Synagogue, shining like a luminous pearl in the night sky. And the shops and sidewalk cafés that line the interior of a courtyard once occupied by Jewish laborers, who lived just steps above the textile and paper mills where they worked.

"It's so alive," my friend observes, as we wander through the *Hof,* where young and old are sipping double espressos or slaking their thirsts with pints of local beer. "That's what I like . . . all these people."

I realize then how much I've grown to care for this small, eccentric man whose company I've kept for a few short days.

Berlinerstrasse . . .

flowering linden trees

fill the night air

The Kindness of Strangers

Perhaps the presence of my mother and me dining in a virtually empty hotel restaurant is what prompts Chef Lou to extend an offer of dessert and coffee. Regardless, my mother, who likes attention from men, is in her element. "Thank you," she says, nodding coquettishly to the chef.

Chef Lou, who flew in to cook at an Oklahoma City food show, tells us he expected this trip to be uneventful. "I've done thousands of these shows," he says. But finding a few hours at the end of his workday, he decided to visit the memorial to 168 men, women and children who lost their lives on April 19, 1995.

The collection of 149 adult- and 19 child-sized bronze-and-glass chairs representing the victims of the Murrah Federal Building bombing seems to float above the adjacent reflecting pool. At sundown the chairs' glass bases take on a soft, eerie glow illuminating the names of the dead. "Such beauty from such sadness," Chef Lou observes.

We finish our coffee and say our goodnights. As I wheel my mother through the hotel lobby, Chef Lou catches my eye and nods before turning back to his plate.

memorial

so many empty chairs

touched by moonlight

Sacred Ground

Just before sunset, I head toward the memorial. A fence borders one corner of the site, where people have left tokens—baseball caps, ribbons, poems, postcards—in tribute to the victims. Beyond that, there's the reflecting pool, guarded on both sides by the Gates of Time, two monumental walls: the east gate set at 9:01 a.m., before the bombing occurred; the west gate set at 9:03 a.m., just after the incident.

At the site's other border is a large elm called the Survivor Tree. During the past one hundred years, it's survived Dutch Elm Disease, tornadoes and droughts, and, most recently, the shock and aftershock of a four thousand-pound bomb. Park rangers say that debris from the bombing had to be hand-picked from the tree's branches; its roots excavated from the rubble and given "breathing room"; and surgeons called in to slowly nurture it back to health and make cuttings of its offspring—saplings given as gifts to dignitaries and purchased by visitors who bear witness not to destruction but to renewal and rebirth.

I think about Chef Lou's words from the night before. About the visit he'll be making in a few weeks as he travels across the Atlantic to visit his aging mother. About the conversation he'll have as they sit down to Seder dinner.

change of seasons

I catch myself talking

to the wind

Melting Snow

At first, I'm not sure what I'm seeing. But Mother has seen him too. She points to a gaunt man standing beneath a downspout next to an old Mom and Pop motel with a half-collapsed roof and weathered vacancy sign. He's dressed in flimsy trousers and a cotton shirt. Melting snow pours out in a waterfall that cascades over his head, his torso, his arms, his spindly legs. He scrubs himself with gloved hands.

another setback

on this road I travel

without you . . .

I try to imagine

my place in the world

Drive-by

In Vicksburg, Lenore kindly offers to give us a drive-by tour of her hometown's antebellum charms. I like her immediately. Even more so when I find out between pauses in our around-town exploration of stately mansion houses and miscellaneous depositories of Civil War-era musket balls just how similar our paths are.

Like me, Lenore returned home from life in a larger city to care for her aging mother. She, too, was once married, long ago, is divorced, childless. And more to the point, like me, she clearly adores her mother.

"Such a pretty girl," my mother says to me later when we're tucked into the queen-sized, four-poster bed that's our allotment for a night in one of Vicksburg's historic bed-and-breakfasts. "I don't understand why some man hasn't snapped her up."

This last comment, like many of my mother's, is an out loud thought, not meant to be answered. It is, in fact, a statement that parallels her increasing concerns for me. "What will you do when I'm gone?" she's asked more than once in recent months. I try to reply as wittily as possible, which is to say not well.

"I'll cry a lot," I say more often than not.

"Then what?" My mother is not easily deterred.

"I'll cry some more."

military park—

among the white-washed stones

a single woman

bids us goodbye, soldiering

on from bloom to harvest

Defining Moment: 9/11, 2001

The fourth or fifth time I speak with my sister in Omaha she tells me she's just come up from the basement where she filled all her family's thermoses with water before climbing back to turn on the dishwasher, take a shower, dry herself off, and dress herself in black.

"I'm going to wear black for as many days as there are victims," Sara says, her voice determined but breaking.

It is the breaking voice I recognized from that morning's first call when I'd stumbled to interrupt the message Sara was in the process of leaving. Grabbing the phone's receiver, I knew, even before she said anything more, that something unspeakable had happened.

On my 19-inch television screen, a nightmare was unfolding. Only it wasn't a nightmare. I was awake, safe, in my home in Arkansas, sinking deeper into my mother's easy chair, the remote clenched in one hand as I watched a plane fly into the north tower of New York's World Trade Center before exploding into flames and black mushroom clouds of smoke.

Seventeen minutes later, the second tower, like its twin, is hit—molten glass-and-steel becoming showering ash. And then the video replays begin.

names of the dead . . .

for a moment the fog

parts and rises

winter night a litany of falling stars

The River Road

Dressed in a working man's period costume, my guide comes from a long line of sharecropping Creoles who worked the sugar cane land no one else wanted—bottom land, close to the river, susceptible to flooding and malaria—for generations. It's clear that mansion house life is as foreign to him as it is to me; still, he's well-versed in the house's accoutrements, and is quick to point out such oddities as the gilt-covered "fly"— an elaborate pulley-driven harness used to levitate a small slave boy above a massive table during dinner service. From his improvised aerie, the acrobatic servant swung back and forth overhead, fanning the heads of plantation diners with ornately dyed ostrich feathers.

But it's the bedrooms I find most interesting. My guide points out the mattresses' ticking—not the luxurious down feathers I'm expecting, but dried leaves stripped from the cane fields. Here, too, are glass receptacles, shaped like bells, which were heated first, then placed strategically over the prostrate torsos of those unfortunates who believed their maladies—from chest colds to bronchial infections and worse—could be coerced from failing bodies and trapped inside the glass vials as if by osmosis.

on the road

a river of memories . . .

tangled moss

clinging to the live oaks

with parasitic beauty

Blushing Bride

We catch up with Frank and Beverly over a lunch of cold chicken salad at our Little Rock hotel. Frank graduated from the University of Oklahoma's law school alongside my parents. He and his wife went on double-dates with my mother and father, hopping the trolley that connected the college town of Norman to Oklahoma City for occasional nights out when they were all courting.

> blushing bride—
>
> Hiroshige's Mt. Fuji
>
> her only trousseau

I mention our recent trip to Oklahoma City, commenting on the memorial site to the victims of the Murrah Building bombing. And the elm— the one they call the Survivor Tree—that remains standing despite the devastation. The church the tree stands across from, says Frank, is where he and Beverly were married. "You remember, don't you, Jeannie?" he asks my mother. "You and Perry were both there."

"That was a long time ago," Beverly says. "More than fifty years."

"Sixty," Frank adds. "Almost sixty-five."

Then Frank, seated diagonally from my mother, glances over at her and exclaims, "You'd never know it by looking at Jeannie. She looks just like a young bride." He punctuates "bride" with an enthusiastic drawl that lingers in the air above our plates like a shimmering bubble: the kind I often see my mother create on a whim, dipping a plastic wand into a jar of soapsuds, to fill our living room with childlike wonder.

"Oh now," my mother demurs. But she's beaming. Under the table, her crossed leg is swinging with abandon.

> old trees
>
> says the cherry master
>
> hold the souls
>
> of the dead who live on
>
> to see blossoms dancing

Winter's Light

It's late January—one of those rare, balmy winter days that occasionally happens in Arkansas—and my mother and I have taken advantage of the break in weather to take a day trip to one of our favorite places.

We've been making the trek to this mountain town—together and individually—for almost three decades. Its Victorian architecture and cobblestone streets always captivate us, no matter the season. But winter—when it's quiet—without tourists—makes us feel this is our own private playground. Today, we've wandered through the few shops that are open; ambled through a woodland chapel; driven to the panoramic crest overlooking the surrounding valley. We're happy.

As we head west out of town, winter's light—the kind that's clear and golden and makes you want to testify—bathes us and the receding streets with more warmth as the sun begins to set. It's then that my mother, one eye to the future, says to me, "Perhaps you can live here." *When I'm gone, she means, but she doesn't have to say more.*

soapsuds . . .

mother tells me how

she'd like to die

Sant'Agnese in Agone

It's said her skull rests in the church that's named for her—a darkened place ignited by a sea of votives and the perpetual smell of incense and must. According to legend, St. Agnes, an early Christian, was persecuted and martyred at the age of twelve for refusing to marry any number of wealthy statesmen. As punishment, she was dragged naked to a brothel in order that her status as virgin—a status that forbade her execution—might be reversed. Along the way, Agnes' fervent prayers resulted in a miraculous sprouting of tresses which created a Godiva-like covering to conceal her nudity. The men who were to ravage her were, likewise, miraculously struck blind. Undaunted, the powers-that-be tied poor Agnes to a stake, but the woodpile she stood on failed to light, forcing her executioner finally to draw a sword and behead her; her blood leaving a telltale trail that stained the piazza's narrow streets.

marble gods

at play in a fountain

built by Bernini . . .

one baroque heart breaking

free from a pagan past

St. Agnes' Eve

My father has a penchant for spouting snippets of British poetry when it suits him, which is often, his small repertoire of Chaucer and Shakespeare and Keats recycled with each season. He bellows out one of his favorite winter lines, shaking off the bitter chill of an Oklahoma January as he steps into the warmth of our kitchen. His oversized galoshes already unbuckled, still dripping with precipitation as he leaves the heavy weight of oil leases and plains' snow and ice temporarily behind him.

He's a big man, my father. The timbre of his voice mellow and deep. It's a voice that earned him a cross-Atlantic trip to pre-war Germany when he was just a teenager. A golden voice. Oratorical. The kind that breaks down the world of saints and sinners in a measured way, line by line, year after year.

> yahrzeit candle
>
> from my lips to God's ears
>
> your memory

Note: In the Jewish religion, a yahrzeit candle is lighted on the eve of the anniversary of a person's death and burns continuously for 24 hours as a memorial to the passage.

Defining Moment: July 20, 1969

It was the culmination of an era. But of course we didn't know that. All we knew was that we'd never look at the heavens in quite the same way. Never find ourselves staring up at the moon and wondering if the outline of a man we saw there was real or imaginary. Never ask ourselves if he really could send us peace and prosperity and happiness and the sea of tranquility, whatever that might be. Never lie down on a hot summer night, rays of light streaming through an open window, and question the probability that we would wake up, happily-ever-after in a true love's embrace. Never doubt all that.

sweet sixteen

waltzing with my father

on a moonlit night

total eclipse viewing the moon without you

All-Stars

When I read what your student has to say about you, I'm humbled. Clearly, she loved you. But that doesn't surprise me. I can't count the number of people—women, mostly—who've told me how much they loved you during the weeks and months since your death.

At first I was touched by the outpourings. But soon, I admit, it made me uncomfortable to listen as strangers gushed over you. As if I were their confessor, someone who would welcome their confessions, perhaps even offer absolution. Or worse, as if I wasn't standing there at all as they professed their love for you, when all I could do was smile and nod and say *thank you*. Until I couldn't.

Yet here I am, reading this confessional. And weeping, as much for her as for me, when she writes of the day you told your class about stars. About how their matter continues to light up the sky long after they've exploded or imploded or simply relinquished their place to the night. About how all you have to do is look to see them still shining.

    meteor shower . . .

    we name each falling star

    for the loved ones

    who pass again before us

    this bright cloudless morning

Lost & Found

At first I think they're named for poets—the kind who spread epic tales of adventure, love and power throughout the land. But then I learn they were named not for their songs but for their stripes. And I feel naïve; diminished, somehow.

Until now, when I hear my calling . . . and yours . . . in their mnemonic cry: *Who cooks for you? Who cooks for you all?* And I have to smile as I remember standing beside you, watching as you stirred our broth to a simmer before offering me the first sample from an oversized spoon.

backwoods . . .

the narrow path of barred owls

fed by the night

Why I Overtip at the Truck Stop

Because the waitress never asks why I'm eating alone. Or what I do for a living. Or what kind of week I've had.

Because she doesn't blink at what I'm wearing, even though I'm dressed in a faded denim shirt that's clearly too large for me. With a small tear at the top of the back pleat. And buttons sewn on the right side, instead of the left. And sleeves rolled up more than once to keep the cuffs from obscuring my fingers.

Because she instinctively knows my back story.

Indian summer

drowning my sorrow

in a fresh cup of Joe

Past Perfect

It never is, you know. Perfect. Even if you left behind one life to run towards another. Even if you had been happier before . . . or after. Or even somewhere in between.

The day of your death you said, *It's all about timing.* Using the present, even though your eyes already were cast on the future. Or was it the past?

If we had met before, would our life together have been simpler? Or just different. Somehow.

    taking flight

    over the Atlantic

    I make my way

    toward guttural declensions

    my ancestors used to speak

Defining Moment: March 24, After the Ides, Post-Solstice, the Lenten Season

The day my mother turned 48, she suddenly appeared before my fourth-grade class—her signature red hair and violet eyes flashing like neon—to hand out homemade cupcakes from a silver tray. I was nine, but instantly I felt older, wiser, more admired, more cherished. So when you asked me to pick a day— that morning, when I'd grown impatient with you for dancing around a date we might call our own— that morning when I'd taken off the ring you gave me and tried to thrust it back into your hand— that day when you told me to put the damn thing back on and never take it off again, my reply was emphatic. *She used to give me her birthday*, I told you. *We could share it.*

full circle

wearing your wedding band

on my right finger

Reentry

4-28-2013. Four months into it your journal stops abruptly with *Bad ending to a good day*. Then seven months later you pick up with a whole page of entries: *Beautiful woods this morning. Great cup of coffee. . . "Dawg" happy to see me. . . Counting my blessings!*

You carry on with your accounting through sleet and fog, burst pipes and a power outage. Until just before Christmas when you write, *Feeling great today. . . .* Then more silence. And then more.

8-15-2016. Found your harmonica and a small leather notebook squirreled away in a drawer under a nest of abandoned cords. Even now I hear your voice telling me not to mess with your stuff, but I can't help it. When I open the journal's cover, I see your name printed in large letters on lines beneath "This book belongs to—". . . . I turn each page and read your entries before turning back to the beginning to add my name beneath yours.

> gaps
>
> in your journal—
>
> knowing the way
>
> one thing leads to another
>
> I write the next page for you

returning the owl's call windchimes

Oculus

It's easy to think of Jupiter and Mars and Venus being as at home here as in the heavens. Soaring to one hundred-ninety feet, the Pantheon dwarfs mere mortals. I turn my eyes from the skylit dome to see a young couple backdropped by a colossal column of marble; their casual attire—oversized sweaters loose over shapeless khakis—belies their intensity. The boy has his arms draped around the girl; his back huddled against ancient, veined stone. They seem, in this room full of strangers, like the only ones present; solitary and small, yet, somehow, capable of occupying the entire space, claiming it as their birthrights.

third niche from the left—

Raphael's god's eye view

of perpetual light

Pendant Power

Even as a child I admired the cameo, not merely for its beauty but for some incontrovertible spirit it seemed to embody. My mother's pairing of the necklace with a simple black dress reserved for birthdays and anniversaries heightened the stone's power. That my father had traveled halfway around the world to find the pendant added to its charm.

"Your father was hopelessly romantic," my mother would say of the gesture.

Cupid and Psyche . . .

beneath Vesuvius

I find myself

whispering the story

to my love-struck heart

Grand Tour

Buried under two feet of ash during Mount Vesuvius' 79 B.C.E. eruption, the lost city of Pompeii lay as still as death until mid-seventeenth-century archaeologists began exhumations. The resurrection revealed a once-thriving Roman colony, its daily life centered around the forum (with temples to Apollo and Jupiter) and the nearby baths, the latter regulated by underground furnaces that provided lukewarm, hot, and cold dips in pools to stimulate circulation.

With Pompeii's reemergence came a stream of tourists that continues, along with excavation of the site, to this day. But at the height of the eighteenth-century Grand Tour, English visitors often returned home with cameos of Apollo, the god of music, or Diana, goddess of the hunts, carved from Mount Vesuvius' abundant lava. Less expensive than more traditional cameos of shell and agate, the carvings were proof of a traveler's journey to a place that, although unearthed, remains an enigma.

love charm . . .

the brothel's graffiti

etched in stone

Love Letter to a Dead Poet

Everyone loved you. Even those you made it your business to cow: bullying them with that voice that could fill three football fields; that linebacker's body; those eyes that could spark a smoldering fire. You loved posturing. Dressing in the cabled threads of an Irish fisherman's sweater. The frock coat and string tie of a country singer. Holding court over pliable minds with one Socratic wave of your cigarette. Postulating theories as if they were facts. Peppering language with expletives meant to shock anyone not prepared to do battle with the fretted words of Dickey & Welty, O'Connor & Faulkner—Southern icons whose secret handshakes we learned to covet as much as God's singular electrifying touch.

once you told me

I danced like

a periodic sentence . . .

it's true enough is

never enough

In My Inbox . . .

Notice of a star-studded auction: The remaining estate of the "World's Most Glamorous Grandmother," including a letter (estimated to sell for $50,000) that begins "Dearest Kraut."

Ernest and Marlene (there's no need for last names, is there?) met in 1934 on the Ile de France ocean liner when the Hemingways (Papa and Pauline) were on a junket. The tempestuous screen siren—so much more glamorous than his fresh-faced second wife—immediately caught Papa's eye, and the two maintained a letter-writing romance until Ernest killed himself almost 30 years later.

Liner note: King of Tight Prose and Silver Screen Queen caught in flagrante delicto, engaged in titillating chit-chat.

Thirty-one years after Hemingway's suicide, his "little Kraut" died in her Paris apartment at the age of 90. By then, say biographers, she lived the reclusive life of a seasoned alcoholic addicted to painkillers.

Obituary tidbit: In her twilight years, the self-avowed atheist converted to Catholicism. Marlene was buried with the St. Christopher medal she cherished.

Timing is everything. Hemingway once told a friend that he and Marlene were "victims of unsynchronized passion."

Translation: They never went to bed with one another.

Still, there's the letter—one of 50-odd letters the couple exchanged during their romantically charged friendship.

pheromones . . .

the stale remains of smoke

and mirrors

skipped generations the Irish in her eyes

Milestones

Just north of St. Louis the August heat seems even more oppressive. The rich riverbed giving way to a monotonous play of farmland stalked by endless rows of ripening grain. Somewhere along the road a simple metal marker fractures the flattened landscape. The small, sun-burnished sign forces me to squint to read the words: MOTHER JONES HOME.

>lace-curtain Irish . . .

>hand sewing the hem

>with a blind stitch

>I measure the distance

>between mother's last breaths

I had assumed that "Mother" Mary Jones—Irish immigrant and union organizer—had been bred with coal dust in her bones. Teacher. Dressmaker. Yellow fever stole her family. Fire, her livelihood.

>rising phoenix—

>who is this spirit

>who won't stay down?

>sticking to the union . . .

>hanging on for dear life

Mother Jones, adjusting her attire and birthdate

to assume a more matronly persona, became the voice of striking miners, their wives, their children. Some dubbed her the "grandmother of all agitators"; others called her "the miners' angel."

Alone in my borrowed car, I pledge to follow the marker on my return home. But I never do. I look for but can't find it.

     north by northeast

     a splinter of geese flies

     far from this heat

     I too ponder

     how I'll leave this earth

Casseroles and Corn

It's a strange trip, partly because I am imposing myself with a vengeance on people I barely know: my cousin Art, a small man nearing retirement and the keeper of the family archives, and his wife, a tiny, round woman named Vera. They are both kind in their way, opening their door to a virtual stranger, but the opening of that door leads to discoveries not altogether welcome.

Out of Pandora's Box comes an avalanche of revelations. First and foremost is the understanding I gain of my father's position within the family. None of his cousins seem to have cared for him. One woman, Art's older sister, in fact, has such unpleasant memories of my dead father that she refuses on principle to meet me.

"He used to tease her," Art says, somewhat apologetically adding that his sister is a bit *imbalanced*. The cause of Art's ruling on this sister's emotional state seems to center on the fact that she never married. Her latest breach of sanity, however, is that—well in her seventies— she has set off by herself on a cross-country trek to visit friends in Arizona. "She didn't even *tell* anyone," one of my kinswomen moans.

reunion tour—

between casseroles and corn

I find my voice

dishing about car wheels

and the call of the road

Three-quarter Time

Orphaned at an early age, my father spent part of his childhood in his grandparents' house on Koch Street in an immigrant neighborhood not far from the town bandstand where my great-grandfather the musician hiked, bass viol in tow, to perform on summer evenings. Today the house is a rambling, dingy-white clapboard that sits on a barren corner lot once planted with the kind of fragrant perennials associated with our grandmothers' gardens.

Camera-in-hand, I stand, watching, waiting, thinking I might capture some long-lost image; that through some magic transformation of the eye, my lens might transpose the house I see before me for the house my father, his father, his father's father and mother once filled with sound and life. I close my eyes and try to imagine the swell of stringed instruments rising and falling under rosined bows that covered the parlor's chairs with the fine, soft dust of music.

Then I look up at the house's second story— where my great-grandfather's workroom was lined with tables for rolling handmade cigars from sweet, golden flakes of cured tobacco. The second floor is bordered by a railed catwalk, and I find myself wondering how many times my great-grandfather must have taken a turn outside the confined rooms of a cigarmaker to see the tops of linden trees blooming, to smell air untouched by tobacco, to hear, perhaps, the strains of a

Viennese waltz drifting from some far-off place in his imagination.

ghost moon . . .

the three-quarter time

of a lost generation

Strangers on a Train

Traveling through the fairy tale world of the Rhine Valley, I watch old castles rise from the surrounding mountainside as I try to reconcile their charm with the shadow of history. It's then that a woman across from me offers up a piece of her own history—as if it were a tidbit she might serve with tea or coffee.

The woman is on the far side of middle age. Her face passive, blank, unfurrowed. She seems to me the epitome of the word *Frau*. Round. Blonde. Harmless. She stares down at her silent hands. When she looks up, she directs her eyes to some place in the distance. "My father," she says, "was in the war."

She speaks her words softly, matter-of-factly, and yet they feel like blows to my stomach, my head, my heart. "I was just a child then," she adds, looking into my eyes, pleading with me to understand her side of an unspoken, perhaps unspeakable, story.

somnambulist—

the Rhineland's sleeping beauty

ringed by barricades

of briars and brambles

as she wakes from her dream

cobwebs never easy letting go

After the Funeral

On the night flight back to Manhattan, I replay our last phone conversation. Hear the slurred speech from his deathbed as he asks if I'll be coming home soon. The pain in his voice when I try, as jauntily as I can, to tell him my plans— plans both of us know won't accommodate a face-to-face reunion.

Now, miles above the darkened ground, I practice what I might have said to him if I'd had one final chance, repeating the words like a mantra. *Thank you for opening your heart to me. For loving me. Thank you . . .*

> landing strip
>
> the skeletal path of light
>
> on the runway

The Gathering

It starts like this. The guests begin to gather. The gathering grows into a circle of well-wishers. Friends and strangers. Meeting. Greeting. One question leading to another. And another, as small talk swells into more small talk. After a while, someone speaks the name of a person from your past. A person you remember. Vaguely. Your childhood neighbor. A person who, you recall, had a father who occasionally strolled out into his back yard, across from your back yard, dressed only in an undershirt and boxer shorts. A chain link fence divided you from him.

And her. His daughter. The person you never took the time to know. The person who you discover, quite by chance, died some years ago. Suddenly.

bonfire flames curling into darkness

Bush Tucker

At dinner, I find myself surrounded by tourists from a geriatric bus tour who've traveled from the seaside town of Adelaide to see the Outback before it's too late. Seated next to me is a soft-spoken woman named June. She has clear blue eyes; silvered hair she's swept up into an immaculate beehive; and the kind of timeless beauty most women hope for as they age.

Between courses—a watery soup, a lackluster tossed salad, a presentable corned beef with cabbage and small roasted red potatoes—June tells me about her life. How her husband died a few months ago from cancer. How their only child, a daughter, lives a continent away in Kuala Lumpur. How much she misses them both, as well as her two grandchildren—a boy and a girl. How friends told her she needed to be with other people. That she should experience a bit of her own country. That a change of scenery would do her good.

By the time the apple crumble arrives, we're almost family.

> particle of light . . .
>
> the gentle blurring of hands
>
> when we wave farewell

Pillow Talk

Once, long ago, I meet a man who has taken to traveling wherever he goes with his best suit of clothes. Like a boy scout, he is, he says, in "be prepared" mode—ready, as soon as he receives a phone call summoning him home to his mother's funeral.

"She's practicing death," he tells me, demonstrating how she pulls the covers tightly over her head just before she falls asleep each night.

> winding sheet—

> he models the leather coat

> he bought in Rome

Confessions from The Mother Road

Just because I'm pushing my mother in a wheelchair (a small one, easily collapsible, handy for traveling) doesn't mean she can't walk—just not fast enough to keep up with me. She also can talk. And hear. And see. And up until recently she has had sex on a more regular basis than I have.

Route 66—

the museum's black-and-white

checkerboard flooring

skywriting all the disappearing words between us

Last Picture Show

Most nights, I find my mother incessantly reading—a pencil and pad at her side for capturing quotes she likes or words she wants to look up later. But not long before she dies I drag myself out of bed in the middle of the night to see her surrounded by cartons of old photos. "What are you doing?" I ask, like someone who's been stun-gunned into forming the most banal and obvious question.

"I'm looking at pictures."

"At four in the morning?"

"So?" she asks, without looking up from her task, and immediately I hate myself for sounding overly controlling. "If I don't write on the back of them, how will you know who they are later?"

"Later than this?"

"When I'm gone," she says, licking pencil lead with her tongue before turning one old photograph over to write down the appropriate names and approximate ages of people forever frozen on the paper's glossy side.

mother's trunk—

among her old love letters

a trace of wild rose

dusting my fingertips . . .

her long-buried secret

Reading by Moonlight

The last survivor in a family of thirteen children, my mother has—if not a first-name—at least more than a passing acquaintance with Death. It's an Old School relationship, the wake of each subsequent relative marked with the same kind of attentiveness given to other significant milestones: baptisms, graduations, weddings. Over the years, when one of my aunts died, my mother and her remaining sisters rallied like schoolgirls to deck out the deceased in finery worthy of a cotillion, putting last-minute touches on hair and make-up before gathering to take one final snapshot of their loved one for posterity.

    in her album

    my aunt wears a crooked smile

    familiar enough

    to remind me why we all

    carry on despite ourselves

In addition to her siblings, my mother's outlived two husbands; a son; infant children—one stillborn—several others, miscarried. She knows death's hand much more intimately than I do. That, I can't know as I lie down for a few hours' rest, is about to change drastically.

life line/love line?

how was I to recognize

all the answers

until you taught me how

to read by moonlight

Nothing More . . .

remains of the house her father built close—too close—to the tracks. Not the wraparound-porch where she and her sisters perched like a charm of songbirds. Not the wooden swing hung from the porch ceiling. Or the morning glories that climbed the whitewashed columns.

Neither is there a sign of the plot her mother tended, coaxing harvests of turnips and tomatoes and okra from the red dirt clay. Nor the chickens that ranged there, beloved as the most beloved, until they are called one by one to grace another table. Nowhere the steady hum of her sisters' many voices: laughing, crying, whispering, sighing their way through hardscrabble winters and white-hot Oklahoma nights.

homecoming . . .

the high lonesome sound

of a passing train

Blue Moons

Sometime past midnight, I wake suddenly. When I enter my mother's room, her breathing is ragged. The tissue she holds to her mouth is covered with blood.

We spend the remainder of the night in Intensive Care. No one has stopped me from taking up bedside residence in a three-quarters-length chair clearly designed for more sporadic visitations. During these hours, I hear a crash cart being raced to a nearby cubicle—doctors barking orders, nurses responding, machines whirring. Then, the unmistakable sound of a flat line alarm as footsteps retreat, heavier and much slower than before. Minutes later, the wheels of a gurney echo off linoleum.

I hover above my mother's chest to make sure she's still breathing. I stay that way until long after daybreak.

one breath becoming two blue moons

Making the Rounds

By the time I get back to the hospital, my mother's awake and the doctor has made his rounds. "Put some lipstick on," my mother says before I have a chance to say anything.

I tell her that I don't care about lipstick, but I take her observation as a sign that she's feeling more like herself. Then she tells me what's behind her concern over my appearance: the *doctor.* "He might not be married," she whispers, conspiratorially.

"I see," I say, planting a lipstick-smeared kiss on one side of her face.

who will call me now

by my other name . . .

soft rain falling

Vigil

A stream of visitors travels to my mother's bedside. At first it's my sisters, along with their children. Intermittently, cousins come, nieces, neighbors, church friends, members of her book club. She sits up, chatters gaily with each one, drinks tea, eats small portions of sweets or soups we carry to her room in an endless procession. Except for a noticeable weakness, she is, as always, the life of the party.

One by one, my three sisters return to their lives, their work, their families. One of them, conflicted, is torn between staying or leaving. I convince her to go home to her husband and tell her I'll call her, daily. Selfishly, my motives are ulterior: I want to spend whatever time remains, alone, with my mother.

Over the next week, the visitors change: hospice workers—nurses, health care aides, social workers—replacing more familiar faces. My mother becomes progressively weaker.

> death watch
>
> the sleeping dog
>
> at her bedside

Throwback

This is my sister's story. My sister, who carries the genes of our mother's grandmothers—Miriam and Polly and Mary—in her face, in her arms, legs, feet, hands. My sister, whose skin is red, like a sunset that bleeds into the Oklahoma sky on summer nights. My sister, who glows with the light of a thousand fireflies.

shadowland

the name mother calls out

from her deathbed

Plainsong

I ask my mother what, if anything, she thinks lies beyond this life. She pauses for a moment before comparing life—and death—to a train ride. "You get on, and, at each new destination," she says, "the scenery changes. Some of it looks familiar. Some of it doesn't. But it's always changing. And it's always exciting. And you just keep going until you get to a place you've never seen before. And then the train stops . . . and you know you've reached the end of your journey."

reading Shakespeare

I try to teach my students

metaphor . . .

shaken by the music

of bare ruined choirs

Through Darkness

When the preacher arrives, I prepare to leave him and my mother alone; however, I soon discover this is impossible. My mother's increasing weakness has made it difficult for her voice to be heard when the listener has less than keen hearing. My mother, it is clear, can hear him perfectly, but, when she utters a response to his questions or adds an extemporaneous comment, he's at a loss to understand her.

"She says she wants to thank you for your kindness," I interject at one point, relaying my mother's message to him like a third-party translator.

The preacher nods and takes my mother's hand.

"She's worried about what will happen to me," I add.

At this remark, the preacher's face registers an element of surprise. When he looks from my mother to me, I have to turn away before I continue.

"She wants to know if you'll look after me . . . when she's gone."

And there it is. With the force of one compressed sentence, my mother's concern—not for herself but for me—has landed squarely in both the preacher's lap and mine, and there's no easy way to pass off what is, essentially, a hot potato.

power outage—

side by side we monitor

the sky . . .

each flash of light revealing

another way through darkness

city lights homesick for the stars

Ground Zero

Seven months after 9/11, I book a flight to the city I once called home. It's my first trip to New York in two years. My first plane ride since my mother died a week-and-a-half after her 87th birthday. It is, I tell myself, a pilgrimage—to connect with old friends, to stomp through familiar neighborhoods, to discover what's different and what's remained reassuringly unchanged.

In the city before, during and after September 11, Rosemary anticipates my wish to visit Ground Zero. "I knew you'd want to go," she tells me before I leave for New York. "I want to go with you."

On the site's platform, I turn my eyes to the skyline, hoping for a glimpse of what used to be. Instead, I find testimonials. Bandannas tied to chain link. Notes etched into plywood. Flowers spilling out of plastic water bottles stapled to scaffolding. Countless small tributes.

Afterward, Rosemary and I climb stairs to a second-floor Houlihan's and order martinis. From our table overlooking Wall Street, we see throngs of business suits mingling with T-shirted tourists. "I don't know what to toast," my friend says finally.

ground zero—

one long-stemmed rose dangling

from a makeshift wall

Circle Line

From the moment we board, the ship seems electrified by language. Japanese, German, Italian, French. All superimposed by our guide's Bronx English. A melting pot of indistinguishable words vying for attention. Charging the sky before easing into the sweet release of universal *oohs* and *aahs* as seagulls dance a mirrored tango. Hovering above the Hudson's reflected surface. Chattering to no one in particular.

> twilight cruise—
>
> a moment of silence
>
> as we pass the site

Death Song

The night before my mother dies, her voice—once so resonant—has diminished to less than a whisper. At one point, she sits up straight against her pillows and asks me for cake. I'm thrilled since, for days, she's shown a complete lack of interest in eating anything, her diet reduced to liquids and the ice cubes I grind into chips in a blender I received at a "household" shower to commemorate my long-ago dissolved marriage.

I switch on the boom box I've placed next to her side of the bed. *Beethoven.* Long-stemmed red roses I bought her a few days before are in full bloom in the cut-glass vase on her dresser. After a few bites, my mother pushes her plate of cake away. She lies back down and struggles to say something as I press closer to hear.

> death song . . .
>
> singing her to sleep
>
> one last time

heat lightning the way your hand rests on mine

Defining Moment: November 22, 1963

It's the kind of event that sticks in your memory
bank: the day a sniper shot and fatally wounded
the 35th President of the United States as his
motorcade sauntered through Dallas streets. A
day remembered clearly by almost everyone who
lived through it.

Survivors at the ready to answer the inevitable
Where-Were-You-When questions that network
pundits love to trot out for anniversary specials
before tucking their reels of black-and-white
footage back into the vaults for another decade.

> nursing home call . . .
>
> my sister says she couldn't
>
> save her roommate's life
>
> no matter what she tried
>
> no matter what she did

Caged Birds

    visiting day

    my sister forgets

    blue is a color

This afternoon I'm introduced to the new best friend—a wisp of a woman, dressed head-to-toe in canary yellow. There's a large rhinestone ornament pinned just above her heart. A blue Post-it featuring a list of relatives' names in flowery cursive hangs beneath the jewel. When she walks, the note flutters against her blouse like a dislocated wing.

She pushes one sleeve up to reveal colorful bangles and a white wristband meant to track her movements. *Pretty*, she says, pointing first to her arm, then to me as my sister swoops her up in a tight squeeze. *Who's your best friend?* my sister asks her. Then they both smile broadly—as if they share some unfathomable secret. As if they've known each other all along in some parallel universe I can't begin to see.

    evensong

    a flicker of light

    embracing darkness

Unmarked Graves

I have no photograph to carry with me. Only a few staccato words—scattered like dandelion seeds through generations. So when the sexton asks me if they ever could have had markers, I shake my head, not knowing how the placement of a stone or two might—perhaps—reveal the stories of my mother's grandparents . . . and of the two young grandchildren asleep at their feet.

at Buchenwald

my left hand sets a small stone

near the entrance . . .

the cairn a reminder

of those who've gone before me

Today, underneath a small-town Oklahoma sky, I am a continent away from the fatherland. Come to pay my respects to my maternal side. Empty-handed, how could I know they too would lie in unmarked graves?

buried treasure . . .

mapping each chromosome

from x to y,

and back again

this quiet morning

Letting Go

In Germany it's illegal to scatter a loved one's ashes. So says the commentator of the radio piece on green burial I'm listening to as I drive home from the grocery. It's okay, she says, to cremate. But not to scatter. The cremains must be buried—or kept in an urn placed mindfully on the living room mantel. Or, possibly, oxidized into faux diamonds set into a necklace, bracelet or ring. Although, to be fair, she doesn't discuss this last alternative. One less thing to consider . . .

driving

with your ashes stowed

within arm's reach—

will I ever be willing

to release you to the wind?

Anniversary

It's on my list. Not the one I write down: coffee; cat food; toilet paper. Or the one I carry around in my head: laundry; dishes; floors. But a list, nonetheless, waiting to resurface when I least expect it. Like tonight, when I slide the screen door open for my dog and catch the smell of spring carried inside on a breeze that makes me think of you, again, and of other things hidden away from plain sight. And suddenly my thoughts turn to an old Godiva box I keep on the top shelf of my kitchen cabinet. And how someone might open it one day in hopes of finding a piece of rich dark chocolate. And the look that someone might have when he or she finds instead a cork and the metal cage that once held the cork in place on a bottle of not very expensive champagne. And that someone's chagrin at the irrational hoarding of something so seemingly ordinary.

. . . to have and to hold winter birdsong

Afterword: Invocations for the Living

"It's like that, I guess, when the past come[s] to collect what you owe."
— Esi Edugyan

In coming to the end of *Prayer for the Dead*, readers will understand that Margaret Dornaus has also penned a powerful invocation for living.

The more Dornaus takes us into the past and memory, the further we are drawn into the realms of loss and death, the more we feel connected to our own present existence. Readers cannot help but recall their own histories and the moments that brought them to this point in their lives; that elusive search for meaning and connection. Their very reason for being here. Consider this tanka from her tanka prose "Unmarked Graves":

buried treasure . . .

mapping each chromosome

from x to y,

and back again

this quiet morning

This reminds me very much of the genealogical work I undertook on my own family tree. I was not stopped by an unmarked grave, but by a family secret that denied my father had a biological father different from his half-dozen elder siblings. And that oral history has now died out with all of them. What is this but my own personal unmarked grave, in that I do not know who my own paternal grandfather was, and where he is now resting?

This collection also immediately takes me back to my time as a registered nurse working in aged-care nursing homes, palliative care, and hospice settings, times when I was gifted with memories shared by residents and patients. And in *Prayer for the Dead*, Dornaus gives us a lasting life review that has the ring of truth; a genuine account that has the deepest sense of an honest lived experience in every word. This collection has the potency of a death-bed confession that is delivered with authenticity and compassion.

We appreciate that these prayers for those who have passed, and who are journeying towards crossing over, are made by the living. Indeed, life is richly woven through these haibun and tanka prose. This is a journal about living every moment, and not merely existing until we die. Take the last paragraph and the haiku from the haibun "Winter's Light":

> As we head west out of town, winter's light—the kind that's clear and golden and makes you want to testify—bathes us and the receding streets with more warmth as the sun begins to set. It's then that my mother, one eye to the future, says to me, 'Perhaps you can live here.' *When I'm gone, she means, but she doesn't have to say more.*

soapsuds . . .

mother tells me how

she'd like to die

Dornaus' mother, whose time remaining is thin, has prayers of her own. Prayers for those she will leave behind, and prayers for herself in how she would like to exit this life. But a life that is short on time does not prevent the enjoyment found within a simple sunset. And Dornaus has a gift in being able to capture these ephemeral moments for all time. A sunset, a thought, a passing comment . . . those meaningful soapsud experiences we all have, but so quickly forget.

It is no secret that Dornaus is a gifted haiku and tanka poet, as her work has repeatedly graced countless reputable poetry journals and anthologies around the world. But she is also a gifted lyricist when it comes to working with prose. This is evident in the preceding prose about sunlight so golden that it "makes you want to testify"—one example of many in this collection:

> Venetian blinds transform into the bars of a prison. A summer breeze enters my room without knocking.
>
> *from* "Party People"

. . . my guide comes from a long line of sharecropping Creoles who worked the sugar cane land no one else wanted—bottom land, close to the river, susceptible to flooding and malaria—for generations. It's clear that mansion house life is as foreign to him as it is to me . . .

from "The River Road"

. . . The rich riverbed giving way to a monotonous play of farmland stalked by endless rows of ripening grain. Somewhere along the road a simple metal marker fractures the flattened landscape.

from "Milestones"

. . . I watch old castles rise from the surrounding mountainsides as I try to reconcile their charm with the shadow of history. It's then that a woman across from me offers up a piece of her own history—as if it were a tidbit she might serve with tea or coffee.

from "Strangers on a Train"

This is a poet who inherently understands that the prose within these stories is as important as the individual haiku and tanka they hold. The prose is enticing and delicious in its descriptive imagery. There is a purpose to her sentence construction, and a subtle poetry within her prose that is very in keeping with the quality of the overall piece. It is easy to see that Dornaus respects the adage that the end result is greater than the sum of the parts. Make no mistake: the individual haiku and tanka can be read separate to the prose and are very satisfying. But together, the prose and poems create a far deeper reading experience for anyone who takes this journey.

This collection is also a testament to resilience. The poet has survived much. There has been loss in her personal life. There has been loss within her extended family. Loss in her social sphere. And there has been generational loss for the many who came before her. There is a rich cultural theme running though this narrative. A search for heritage, family, and culture. And Dornaus handles these with a sensitivity that denotes the greatest respect for those who helped shape her own life and experiences:

forbidden words

on the tip of my tongue . . .

her six-pointed star

lace-curtain Irish . . .

hand sewing the hem

with a blind stitch

I measure the distance

between mother's last breath

saying grace—

the cantor's voice rises

in a minor key

memorial

so many empty chairs

touched by moonlight

There are a handful of defining moments in this collection that most mature readers will identify with, as does the author. They include Kennedy's assassination, the moon landing, the bombing of the Murrah Federal Building in Oklahoma, and the devastation of the terrorist attacks on the World Trade Centre in New York City. Dornaus again handles these with the skill of a seasoned writer who reveals just enough so that readers can bring their own emotions to complete her "Where-Were-You-When" pieces of writing:

sweet sixteen

waltzing with my father

on a moonlit night

(1969)

names of the dead . . .

for a moment the fog

parts and rises

(2001)

There are many milestones on the path of every individual. And I am pleased to have reached the marker that has brought *Prayer for the Dead* into my life. This is a work that can teach us much about living, remembering, and how to pass on with grace and dignity:

north by northeast

a splinter of geese flies

far from this heat

I too ponder

how I'll leave this earth

It is my hope, that when my time comes and someone utters a *Prayer for the Dead* for me, it will be a much-loved passage from this compelling collection by Margaret Dornaus.

—David Terelinck, author,
Casting Shadows: Collected Tanka; and,
Slow Growing Ivy

Acknowledgements

To list all the people who have assisted or influenced me in this work would be an impossible task. I am, however, enormously grateful to Marjorie Buettner for her generous foreword, and for her friendship and poetry. I am similarly grateful to David Terelinck, whose afterword speaks volumes about his kind and thoughtful spirit and about his willingness to offer a benevolent service to me at a moment's notice. Heartfelt thanks to them both.

Additionally, I thank Ray Rasmussen not only for providing me with a note for the back cover of this collection but also for guiding me early on. His knowledge, advice and direction were invaluable to me as I learned more about the form and endeavored to write my first haibun.

Thank you as well to Marilyn Hazelton, whose poetry, social conscience, and wisdom grace all those fortunate enough to have made her acquaintance.

Likewise, I am grateful to the many editors who have encouraged and motivated me during the past several years, and to the English-language haiku and tanka community as a whole. From the beginning of my foray into these forms until the present, I have encountered a supportive and welcoming group of individuals whose openness, candor and enthusiasm seem to define the very nature of haiku.

Special thanks to Abigail Keegan for reading and

responding to this manuscript; to Katherine Shurlds for providing clarification concerning a number of grammatical issues; to David Rice for his technical advice and assistance; and to Jacquelyn Stuber for her cover design expertise. Thanks as well to the many acquaintances, friends and loved ones—especially my sister, Sara Seaman, and my late husband Larry—who have enriched my life in countless ways. Their encouragement and devotion inspire me daily.

—Margaret Dornaus
October, 2016

Publication Credits

Many of the poems collected here have appeared in the same or slightly different versions in the following online and print journals: *A Hundred Gourds; Acorn; Contemporary Haibun Online; Frogpond; Haibun Today; Modern Haiku; Notes from the Gean; red lights; Ribbons; Skylark; The Heron's Nest*; and *tinywords.*

Anthology credits include: *carving darkness: The Red Moon Anthology of English-Language Haiku 2011,* Red Moon Press: Winchester, VA, 2012; *contemporary haibun 14*, Jim Kacian, Bruce Ross and Ken Jones, eds., Red Moon Press: Winchester, VA, 2013; *contemporary haibun 15*, Jim Kacian, Bruce Ross and Ken Jones, eds., Red Moon Press: Winchester, VA, 2014; *fear of dancing: The Red Moon Anthology of English-Language Haiku 2013*, Jim Kacian, ed., Red Moon Press: Winchester, VA, 2014; *Journeys 2015: An Anthology of International Haibun,* Angelee Deodhar, ed., CreateSpace, 2015; *nothing in the window: The Red Moon Anthology of English-Language Haiku 2012,* Jim Kacian, ed., Red Moon Press: Winchester, VA, 2013; *The Sacred in Contemporary Haiku*, Robert Epstein, ed., Middle Island Press, 2014; and *With Cherries on Top: 31 Flavors from NaHaiWriMo*, Michael Dylan Welch, ed., Press Here: Sammamish, WA, 2012.

Awards

"years from now"...13
First Place, Tanka Society of America
International Tanka Contest 2011

"blushing bride—"......................................38
Special Recognition, 2012 Fujisan Haiku Contest

"skywriting"..72
Second Place, 17th International Kusamakura
Haiku Competition, 2012

"Caged Birds"..91
An (Cottage) Award, 2014 Genjuan International
Haibun Contest

About the Author

Margaret Dornaus holds an M.F.A. in the translation of poetry—focusing on the works of Neruda and Lorca—from the University of Arkansas. An award-winning poet and non-fiction writer, her food and travel articles are published in a variety of national publications and her Japanese short-form poems appear regularly in international anthologies and journals.

She has taught Culinary Arts, teaches English, and is the book review editor for the Tanka Society of America's journal *Ribbons*. A self-proclaimed late bloomer, her discovery of and appreciation for haibun and tanka prose grew from her interest in blending prose and poetry into a narrative form that could uniquely express her love of nature and the world.

www.ingramcontent.com/pod-product-compliance
Lightning Source LLC
Chambersburg PA
CBHW020920090426

42736CB00008B/726